Songs from the Back Woods of the Mind

Poems

Peter Kirn

Get Fresh Books, LLC
Union, New Jersey

Copyright © 2017 by Peter Kirn

All rights reserved. No part of this book may be reproduced in any manner without written consent except for the quotation of short passages used inside of an article, criticism, or review.

Get Fresh Books, LLC
PO Box 901
Union, New Jersey 07083

www.getfreshbooksllc.com

Cover image: Courtesy of Wellcome Library, London, UK

Cover design & book layout: Leonardo Zuñiga

ISBN: 978-0-692-84378-9

Library of Congress Control Number: 2017934818

Table of Contents

1	1
2	2
3	3
walt whitman would be ashamed of you	4
5	6
6	7
7	8
8	9
9	10
10	11
radio report	12
yesterday the inlets glared at me from a time long gone by	13
prelude to strawberry season	14
the god particle	15
the ant	16
poem for thomas jefferson	17
17	18
18	19
it is an unflowering	20

an assemblage of treasures in the treehouse	21
red-winged blackbird	22
22	23
the pufferfish	24
24	25
poem written in n.r.'s chair	26
26	28
27	29
28	30
mysteries of scale	31
poem in belfast	32
the intimacy with which stone combusts	33
32	34
33	35
34	36
poem for a.m. davis	37
35	38
poem for mara	39
Acknowledgments	40
Note	41

O happy he who can fathom the causes of things,
who's thrown all fear & dogged Fate
beneath his feet...

& blessed is he conversant with the rustic gods...

Virgil

Having heard these words, Arjuna trembled with fear...

Bhagavad Gita

Songs from the Back Woods of the Mind

1

somehow whispering together together
but really believing apart apart at the blue
& black at the edge of the earth in space
currents of dark matter immediately begin to knead
the speckled cosmos one long look
into the algae bloom in the pond & now
i see them everywhere the fluorescent verdant living
calling cards of a greed uniquely human
& the opposite the lights threading out
of my lover's fingers at night
sometimes they're so beautiful i forget
how love makes my senses feel like they're unraveling
then the way she rolls over in her sleep
pulling the cover over her reminds me
time is ever-compounding around the earth that does not rest
so i walk into the kitchen without turning the light on
make a cup of coffee & watch the steam
& at the first crack of daylight i know the nervousness has begun
so i pour my eyesight into some still-sleeping corner
picture the first-day delivery boy with his paintchipped handtruck
the amiable woman turned lone wolf who stalks
& the young planet mumbling spin i am blue

2

the hermit looked her straight in the eye
looked her eye to feral yellow eye
looked her pool of pupil to fleur de lis of wild appleseed
she felt the future like the submersion of coastlines
& the past pulling like merciless workhorses
& when she freed her wrist
& the air finally made it to her mouth
she did not scream as much as glow
she said the hermit was destined to be the most seen of us all somehow
she said there was a tree growing inside her she could not deny
said when they found her old & brittle body
it would already be 3/4 gone into the earth
it would be pulled apart by the roots of trees far older than she was
she knew in the woods down no path
woven into the fabric of pines crudely ordered rows of apples
gnarled prolific long established prevailed
she knew a scent specifically sweet & wet
& some track she wouldn't tell or couldn't
when they captured the hermit
& she's been having these visions ever since
the hermit faded stumpgray as if he'd never lived
& now when the first chill comes in september
& the blush rushes down the sides of the cortlands
on that day i will not touch her

3

begin with the sadly painted almond
eye of the donkey whose foal is buried
at the foot of the banana orchard
that narrows & narrows as she looks for him
in the pasture for days he traces the eye's black makeup
she is in mourning she communicates with him only
out of this eye it is the heart of her skittishness
it is named rico when she says remove it
remove it you must do some things that don't feel right you see
just ask the boy who had to put down the foal
sick with renal failure
put a bullet in him he places the eye in the envelope
of his work clothes & does not forget it
he feels it contains things he cannot understand
it is heavy in his pocket it is her heartbreak
passed down to her from her mother
& her mother before it will need more rain
so he buries it outside it will need a body
so he forms one out of the dirt
he places the eye inside the new body
watches its sad or frightened or glassy or meditating
roll into cosmic looking he leaves the mixture
to the weather when the sun comes up he goes to her
says good morning malika it is gold
today the sea is silver here & inside you the elements are mixing
today you are green & i know it is your wildness
& the eye bursts
& spews out a tangle of roots
a fingerlength sapling he gives it a name
& when the tree is old & guffawing
with the thick old guavas & watching
the breakers as if they were someone else
playing dominoes when he glances back
at the orchard that is part of the secret
he will come to know in the growing of trees

walt whitman would be ashamed of you

i can't imagine him dancing
didn't he like pulling ferries
wasn't it something of a faux pas
for fellas to be dancing with fellas
in his day she must have meant
you're being untrue
to your inner self must have meant
why you're not even ecstatic
in a way that manifests itself
i didn't want him to be ashamed of me
i was studying the dancing teeth of the upright piano
the smoke in the mouth
out the nose of the cigarette pressed below
the mustache of the man playing it
i was playing the beat on the top of my leg
with the heel of my hand
i was nervous i'm a terrible dancer
i told her & she was right
whitman's nervousness is not one of his defining qualities unless he's
evading ginsberg in the penumbras
she was playing the poet angle
she figured i can get this boy to cut it up
if i just bring the father of american letters into it
i'd just as soon leave him out of it
i believe in whitman like i believe in god
always there isn't he
but he wasn't the people dancing
he was the dancing itself & it was whitman in the sparks
that flared out of the hammering in the upright
& if whitman worked a double shift at the creole skillet
he'd be tired too but i wasn't even that tired
i just don't like dancing
i could have lied to her in 100 different ways
could have gotten up
& reproduced the dancing of the solider kissing his gal in times square
with my sliding shoes
shook my hands said hallelujah
could've gone thriller on her
but she was impatient
desperately chasing whitman

into the dance with the middle-aged prowler in the flower print shirt
back away from the bar as for whitman
i thought he might be in the sounds
if i just listened to them with all my heart
she wanted her whitman to be my whitman
but you don't mess with another person's whitman
ginsberg only asked him questions he couldn't ever answer
where are you going
which way does your beard point tonight
& i was tired of questions which foot goes where
& how do i look & feel
so i stayed at the bar
chair hopping toward the piano being played by
some guy saying when you're smilin'
saying mercy with a mustache but really saying
whitman whitman & puffing whitman smoke
into his whitman-stache on his upper whitman
& playing his piano which sang
whitman whitman whitman whitman

5

all the help he can get he'll need
around the next bend the whole earth's throbbing
& the endless demands
are out back behind the thick yellow calluses thinking about rest
they are talking the aches he will come to know like rusting fiddle strings
singing the piles of wood & tangled fencelines
they play that weary creaking depreciating body blues
& eye his bliss
like it is god's own confusion that boy
born too clean & stupid for his own good into this world no doubt
no doubt

6

long after the marigolds
cities began to go up like malignancies
in the countryside   there was no escaping it
& if there was any sign
of our disgust our cynicism
we did not show it
but the bitemarks that morning trailed up my arms
& there was the numbness in her right side
the urine smell of vitriol rose
from the dry reservoirs ringed
with blue like ghost water & the cattle looked
like skeletons wrapped in wet rawhide
& dried in the sun the wild horses decayed
so we fled there was nothing else to do
i put my nose to the oldest books & signs
lost my faith in symbols
& come springtime i planted marigolds as bait for pests
searched for something timeless tireless & thankless
& planned my egress
for there was no use in lying to ourselves anymore
this was going to end ugly

7

the seedlings all over were trembling unprovoked
as my colombian neighbor ana
who collects the eggs & picks the sunflowers outside
of time told me abut the cartographer
who owned the house where i rented a room who died
in a plane crash & left a wife & a young daughter
who moved off the grid & deep summer set in
a week early much to the chagrin of the melon
crop drowning in the south to the delight
of the grasses flashing in the marsh ana said
since the cartographer's death word was the house
had fallen into disrepair   i said it had
if it wasn't flooded it was always some other thing
she shook her head   soaking up
some part of the story with her darkbown eyes
where she was cradling some chicken sure to be killed
by the others speaking to them in spanish
speaking to them in an ocular language
invented of memories
invented of confusion of longing
to know all the tongues of the earth & in
that moment she reminded me of i-don't-know-who
& i believed we were neighbors long before we lived here
she with her mother in colombia me with my love
& we all marched slowly & carefully across the face of time
a wide-eyed people in an unmappable place
stalking something we seemed to instantly know we'd need
at least all four of us to find

8

i dreamt in that gray morning
of mercy & going limp & long long travel
before the crows went for its body
to spare it a few minutes
we covered it with grassclippings
for being part of the farm for a while
the fella i was with said thanks
said picture it in its noblest moment
it was my way flightless for weeks lurking
around the compost pile
out to the southwest in autumn
its eye gone
the way of the wind a stream
of some new element red
beyond red trickling out
of its mouth i had expected a bloodbath but there
was only some muted earthsound & i watched it swollen
wings out-stretched on its downy chest
its belly rotten
with some awful worm
or starving to death
struck by a blade of the windmill
squirming as it was after being
i never was until i crushed the head of a seagull
with a heavy rock
one of these people who dreams of flying

9

love is when she knows the quiet escape to the back fence within him
when she knows the blue world & the edge of the harbor
when they can watch the killdeer limping
& know that each is the heart & each is the nest
when madness is pinging wildly
from creature to excited creature down the shoreline
luring something large & far more effacing & like the ocean
when the moon is illuminated rapidly advancing away

10

i looked up from the exhausted gray
october soil to see the long ragged black tongue
in the sky with the wind billowing beneath it
i marveled then at the resilience of the roots of the dead
until i realized they were still alive
all the more do i see it now
the lovable half-blind illusion of peace
how the insatiable longing between the baker & the world
becomes the dangerousness of the love between the middle son & the baker
i feel the chicken writhing against my cradling
on the day of its slaughter the razor in my left hand
my right thumb & forefinger clearing
its throatfeathers tracing its toothpick jawbone
& i spend these nights awake
imagining the blessing for lightning

radio report

debt crisis bursting into delicate bloom in greece
& civil unrest unfurling in its wake
precipitation blossoming as if it had been dormant
buried invisibly in fleshlike folds in the sky over rockaway
& meanwhile greed was gorgeous
& attracting honeybees to washington
causing slowdowns on the beltway
& the stench of rotting dead was wafting out
of cruise ships run aground in italy
& american drone strikes in pakistan
were spontaneously erupting into furious coloration
& the family was thanking god
for their every blessing when thousands of blood cells
suddenly burst into a sheet of vermillion
in the skies over kabul

yesterday the inlets glared at me from a time long gone by

said honey consider we're all old as water
even the lifetimes of the tall trees
lining the highway between your home in the city
work in the country

pass like the day's chores
planting & tilling
come to believe in the creatures peeking
out from behind the water's winking chasing
each other around the seasons it is their

language you'll believe in
older than the unknown cave poet
older than her rival with her ledger of figures
& when you're lonely

remember the universe wanders through
the vacuum in total isolation
it has no talk
its language flows slowly
out into something more viscous than time

prelude to strawberry season

i

the young leaves leave the trees'
skeletons bare a few more weeks
the work hours are piling up
& collapsing into a weary heap the sun
& farmers wake earlier each
day the first peas & beans are in the ground
the budding lilacs & hands are swollen
& sore but getting tougher & stronger
& we collapse in a weary heap
as soon as we pry our boots off

ii

good morning my love
you are beautiful a beautiful
chaos of atoms
& i miss you
& will return to you soon
& you can tell me
whatever you want
& i will listen
with my ears my
lips my aching
hands & eyes
for the coming of the strawberries

the god particle

i was memorizing the intervals
repeating them when guilt had overtaken me
& interwoven with the god particle i wanted
the weariness of sagging houses
the gymnastic long division of crows
i needed an explanation
for the boy shimmering blue in the galaxy
the constant what's next
for the line of cars mumbling to itself in soot
this one's eyes red with passion it was
to me explained by the solitude of prime numbers
corroborated by the whining weathervane
but the luminous insects had sealed their lips
& codified their displays beyond my knowing
so i waded into the tall grasses
where ticks go for the eyes of now-feral house cats
& found the bird too old to fly in her nest in the brambles
& it was her quiet
& alone
& her just-so-hidden
that was intimate between us

the ant

the skin on the dreamy halfwit sitting
beside the window bristles into a mysterious brail

& they converge on the pulp
spread across the floor like an exit wound

they tune in to the talk
& the seeds like vomiting stones

they know the man is afraid to drink
the groundwater & should be   i know this

they will never know my love for what is buried
beneath the oak trees & sidewalk panels

they will never see the world   the way that i see the world
unless they see the endless maze of tunnels   believe me

i do not hate days on earth & don't
kid myself by cherishing the thought

of peace or death tucked into white sheets
or afternoons spent without toil

poem for thomas jefferson

i had convinced myself the manufacturing world
had nothing to offer us
as if there was nothing beautiful
about the way signals & electricity zapped around over our heads
as if there was nothing beautiful that couldn't be flicked on & off with a switch
nothing beautiful that wasn't beyond our control
as if there was control
as if we weren't in a way being bridled
by the world we had each chosen for ourselves to see
to live in as if this could have gone only one of two ways
the fields or the factory
as if there was no ebb to things
as if there was nothing beautiful

17

i was suddenly unsure of what the cicadas were doing
certainly not all making love or working on it
& the child was singing her prayers like a hole
torn in the night by a lit window
i was at the edge of a cornfield   the end of new england summer
they were out in berkeley like a planet in another galaxy
her cheeks the color of the inner earth squeezing roots
her cheeks the color of sleep where roots grow
where silvery blue taproots grow & spread like lightning
i was the nightbird perched on the outreaching arm of the blade of grass
gone to seed below the windmill dressed in a tight dress the color of the moon
the windmill doing the turn & face waltz with the wind
as confusion passed exactly that way between two speeding automobiles
on the country road headlights like the crosseyed moon
imagining its timestables i watched that confusion
worried it was headed for my brother & his wife
who carried their child like an unknowable pattern
crystalizing into an object the size of an appleseed   the size of a blueberry
the size of a plum   the weight of the moon

18

the granddaughters are named
after fault lines & subduction zones
they whistle twice to call their birthday
which arrives like a weather system
& because they grow inward & quiet
in crowds they turn to the varieties of corn
a modest collection of arrowheads
& when their uneasiness has curled
into a tiny seed
they will always meet back at the old wisteria
for the more they hear the home they cannot see
the more they feel its inner darkness rumbling
the more skeptical of things they feel
the cleaner they become

it is an unflowering

it looks like a wicker baseball
it looks like an oblong birdcage
it looks like a cornfield bundled up & tied off at the top
it is an unflowering
wildflower bound up in a field of flowering
wildflowers & it will probably never seed
& if
in many years we still live
in a world suitable for dainty white wildflowers
chances are that this phenomena
will have worked itself out by then
& the cornfields will lie unfurled
across the hills & we will work
throwing ears by the bushel into the trucks in the midday sun
for all eternity

an assemblage of treasures in the treehouse

imagine a junkyard poet

of whirligigs & windmills gathered in the desert

in search of their lost language

imagine the beautiful neighbor pulling in trashcans

& the soundtrack to the predawn drive through canada coming home

imagine the confusions of shiva's arms entangled

the nuances of flowers recognizing each other in the morning

imagine the tulips deciding to close at night

& the poem dedicated to the line of ants climbing up the wall

imagine the flower that sits on top of the jar full of stones

from a beach on the other side of the country

imagine it's wilting & how

the insects crawling around it in circles

are praying

red-winged blackbird *(for lesley vance)*

a window in several planes
let's call you a portal
situated randomly in space
like a black hole posing as a fleet of cluster flies
floating in the blue world between
the scrub oaks the wild grasses
& the young grape rows marching west
& smaller still your scarlet badge
a slash in the unavoidable
black & sleek & ever-in-motion
into the roaring eye of all things
the smoldering undulating heart of the god of birds

22

years ago after hours
in the five-tinroof fishing town
littered with bud bottles & squidslaughter
the fortune-tellers convened for a nightcap
& a six-foot-two seer named almyra
with eyes like inverted pearls
told me   there's a part of the self that cuts
through y'life like the stream
that divides the southern part of the island
i thought at first it was some lost or dying sadness
she hissed demanded more listening
as a tincture for this cowardice this cleanliness this lying
more attention to the moon she said   when
was the last time you spent the night
gazing up at its underside
with y'head restin' on the belly of the earth
with that she removed a tiny orb
iridescent from inside my forehead
& a measure of thickened blood
from my chest like a sweating hummingbird
& wrung them in her long knuckley hands
i watched her yellow wooden fingernails
as she thumbed the small bottle
where the fluids had collected & shook it   y'see
truth be told you must fuse the two y'self
or else never the two shall meet

the pufferfish

there is an unspeakable thing he holds
so tightly it seems he doesn't know
who he'd be without it he gets up in his sleep
to walk the bush
& mumbles to the trees
about their glowing green eyes
perhaps he's collected my bones from the cobble
beach outside of time between
here & africa
where the cacti kink out of their home in the earth
where the sun & sea polish the bones of the dead
to a smooth porcelain
because he wants me to teach him
to escape because he wants me
to teach him to compress to a form small enough to hide
from all the world
but i cannot teach him these things
i can teach him nothing until he learns
to stare his fear eyeball to eyeball
& expand

24

what is the meticulous knot being
tied by the six moths
weaving in the silent remaining
wilderness at dusk
what is this rise & fall game this spinning
ring they make of where they are
have been & will be   who would have thought it
the moth is omnipresent in its own lifetime
the silence beams it into my ear like a stream of breath
in my 27th year i am part of the unseen root system
of entangled wonder & desire in light
good & clean for drinking
good for sinking in
i believe in thriving in full sun
& prepare my cotyledons
for their spirit is forming
so i tell them about the ferns & the sedges
& the bog & the maples turning
for it's gold in the month of our becoming

poem written in n.r.'s chair

in portland the two young men
try to keep the theater open
they pitch cartoon ideas about the end of the world
juggle checkbooks & characters they're working on
they speak in a code of references
my friend reads wittgenstein derrida works on his impression
of orson welles he says he a masochist
says it's because he's a catholic he likes
to suffer i appreciate the prayer on their wall
beside the amplifiers & mic booms
& stacks of paper about striving for happiness
in a world in which at peace with god
has no analogy
a world of same drudgery & broken dreams it says
true enough i guess i'm just off the farm a few days
my pack full of clothes & poems in this
world at peace with god
has no analogy but there's always a way
to improvise better always another work day
off to the theater off to the brewery the dentist
i grow & grow in their dark attic
i expect moments from any time to appear & they do
i am from last year a ghost in an old town
i anxiously await being lost to the bricks & cobblestones
i love rocking in their chair listening to the analog
clock tick back & forth
i sit in this house & call it life
i worry i wonder
when even this hole in the attic
will run with streams of titus andronicus & blazing saddles & drunkenness
i wonder about these kerouac letters on the bookshelf
how he sounds equal parts naive & neurotic
o world of shame & drudgery
o peace & god & blazing saddles
the only ingredients in dinner are macaroni & cheese
& i'll be long gone by then all of portland buzzing along
the ghost rocking back & forth inbetween the ticks of the old clock
writing poems praising the nervous life

praising the prayer
praising the drudgery
praising god without analogy

—portland maine

26

if you can sound like the back orchard
& move like the canefields you've got it half right
if your sleep is the meaninglessness
that will explain it all   coffee   black   night
black   darkness   glitters   stars   glitter
the love   is in the timing   the peace
is buried in the wheel like the shapes buried in the air
like the sound of the tow truck
buried in the gecko the insect that swallowed
the orgasming couple the nightbird that swallowed
the night   a slow turning that overwhelms you
that you may be lost in it hopeless in it doomed
as the boy & his dead that's why he has come out here
to find them   his heart sagging
like the overripe moon dripping

27

in the rain roaring cascading
down the quarter crescent
of the polyhouse like so many
tails squiggling
heads pointing to the earth
she is feeding the chickens
her child is kicking inside her
lots of standing water
she tells him
it is rushing into the coop
with the one rooster in the battery cage
it is flushing out
of the pigpen
coating the red grain scoop
the donkeys are skittish today she says
in the orchard the orangeblossoms
are coming apart
a crowd of tiny feet is patting
on the dark leaves
of the lime trees
& the yellowing ones
of the grapefruit trees in the lightning orchard
all the earth is flowing
below me little one is full like me is alive
with magnetism listening to the roaring against the skin
on his mama's belly & inside   he is curled around
his own heart

28

it is enormous but as a house not a mountain it is tangled & ordered a utilitarian jumble of brass & copper piping it gleams in no light it works & writhes constantly of its own capacity it produces no object it is full of valves & shutoffs & meters & caps but controls itself its lines are all vertical & horizontal it is rectangular long end down it is right at the corner of messy & neat it is ordered beyond belief as consolidated as could be devised it starts who knows where & ends inside itself only to begin again it pumps what it pumps sometimes so slow it's like the turning of the earth underfoot others it's like a parasite in a man's stomach   it is a beautiful thing   it is mesmerizing   i came upon it one day when i wandered into an empty space devoid of all things   a lonely place where i was not lonely   & the jewel in my side was glowing for it was near   i was enraptured by the machine   it was gorgeous & working & purposeful   i got to my knees to study it it was attached to nothing i touched it   it was weightless   i jumped back   it was clutter   &   i began to search   for a place to put it

mysteries of scale

they have something to do with exposure to light
as if honesty's size were inherently indeterminable
as if there was a patchwork underlying color in shades of absence
as if movements therein were both stable & explicable
& humor was hidden in its own shadow
& centered within the soul was vibrating

poem in belfast

i woke up this morning & drove through
sheets of molten cloudcover
to talk to a stranger about bees
she talked about gravity how foundations
in hives are redundant
she talked about talking to bees
oddness & how it lurks
i passed through the old new england
windows & through blueberry country &
good land for sale the coffee waitress
had a wild high pitched voice
& i imagined her wings moving like oars
& the heart inside her
i teetered on the brink of worry
then watched the fog burn off listened to
it return i prayed to the god of gray things because
it was crawling out of the comb
it was almost mother's day & i was the only man
i saw i could explain how certain moments re-
emerge in our lifetimes how loneliness is
billowing brown spores inside the earth in just such a way
how there is a mathematical precision which nature
takes time unfolding a system
narrowing somewhere
but i look at the harbor & can't say for sure
that i'll ever know it inside & out
can't even say where my devotion lies or
whether i will raise myself well with the hive
no foundation she said & i pictured time elastic
acting upon us
watched the fog envelop the town
there was peace in that
water in all living things

the intimacy with which stone combusts

well past the grid town beginning with s
i drove on the second day
i was lonesome as sleep then
quiet as the widower practicing his music
the size of the atom unfurling wildly
by the time i got to cutler
i was a bellyful of hotdogs & coffee & beer
i was the consistency of pondwater
people sinking in me leaves & pineneedles
rising tiny ethereal particulates suspended
& summer was born & began its dying
& did so in utter silence
& so on the high bluffs an hour deep
into the woods i don't remember if i talked to myself
or if i was silent & only thinking
i was a breath of smoke
i was the movement after the body shivers
in the primitive sacrament i was bound up & hopeless
as a coil of rope i was human that far away
from god who i'd come all this way to see
i was lonely as the ravensounds as the campless travelers
while i waited for the night to break
over the sea the cliffs still clinging to the magenta
& i fed the fire driftwood over the cobble divot
fed it & fed it & got to writing symbols on the
stones with wood turned to char like a boy changes
to his own spirit & wrote a symbol
for my every love said it like a prayerwrote it like one
but it was in tongues
& the stones glowed red
bright red
& were still glowing
when i woke in the morning

32

growing up i couldn't tell you if the door
of my house pointed north or south
but i grew attached to the mid-atlantic
tangerine daybreak in winter
i was a walking talking budding addiction to coffee
developing a fury & cynicism i'm just now learning
to assuage

i was afraid of heavy winds
& called nobodyness convention
& called normality lifelessness

& called my mind my heart
& my desire my love
my fear my difference my alienation
my compulsion to vanish   now

i still wake early to beat the traffic
& study that unchanging place
for it's there i hear the thunder snarling tonight in the cucumber rows
& always on my eastern side
feel the cold sea lapping up

33

he had only ever heard
of fireflies so when he looked out into the night expecting them
it was arranged with empty chairs
like so many shinto portals set up hovering in the meadow
this is how desire evolved to linger like settling particles
his curiosity to hurry like air
it's how the absence of a thing comes to stand for the thing itself
expanding like empty space burst
sporadically & with unfathomable efficiency
into light without heat

34

on the evening of the 10th new moon they arrived here

they said this was part of an interlocking network
of safehouses small farms & homes with secret
compartments on islands & in bordertowns

we welcomed them in

they talked about a long narrow path
to liberation said the sickness was spreading
as if it could not be stopped

& asked as they were leaving
at daybreak my mother
about the autumn olives that grew
at the edge of our pasture they listened
carefully to my brother who turned
over mushrooms in a basket & my grandfather
who wiped grease on his pantleg

they were students of an old old way
& so could see straight
when my sister looked at them with her long hair tangled
with dreams lingering in her eyes like still water

the truth is they were striking out blindly
for some unwavering thing
though we were all ourselves its wavering
& so i whispered nothing as the dawn purpled
& we held each other's anxiousness
to travel directly into it
to face the onslaught
as if it weren't coming for all of us

coming for the polyrhythm of lilac & peony
coming for the nestedness of organics in convention
coming for the carrying capacity of the brood

poem for a.m. davis

many years ago the boy received a letter from a young seeker
it was in a tongue he had never imagined
& contained a great deal of wisdom

the boy had no way though the young seeker
was kind & sagacious to send it & very beautiful besides
her blue eyes like long wells

to respond to this language try as he may
yet he set out to the work the young seeker described
he searched for the darkness of the heart
which he learned had always been

he searched for the whiteness of the whale
& marveled his inner jewel trembling

he searched for the chiaroscuro in the balance
but this was a work he found that would never end

it would evolve in fits of fury or hunger
peace & loss & wrongness wrongness wrongness

he knew he could wait no longer to write
the young seeker no longer young now
so he whispered love into the
mouth of a fish & sent
it swimming off to find her
the fish lived to be very old
& had many adventures
he whispered protection & gratitude into the inner ear of an oyster
& its shell hardened & grew like a great mound of claydrippings

the boy prayed his note would reach the seeker
that she would know what she had done for him

that her existence was always in his mind
that she visited him in his dreams
& that he felt a companionship with her
he would only whisper to the things of the sea

35

    the winding paths form like tributaries
    like a thumbprint the one-story wooden structures & granaries
    dot the hillside & thatched houses steam with foodmaking
          above the pasture sits the crook
          of the crescent moon looming massively
      you should see all the people here
      there is silence leaking through them
      as if they were the dreams of conifers
    their paths are circular but not circles
    connected but not fluid
    fluid but not connected
          the only sound is the wind in the tributaries
          not the dust blowing on the cartpaths though it blows
          not even the girl though she sits
          singing quietly in the grove

poem for mara

the wind is composed of so many circles
i will never grow tired of seeing them

but there is a special one in her niece's eye
like the rings of a planet that is dark & overturned & over

turned again it is a tiny object at sea & lost to
that sea & at its mercy & airless
it is a way of seeing   a gateway that flips

samsara into stillness wonder into fury
stillness into wonder wonder into stillness

that the mind may go forward in some kind of peace
that the heart may grow to the size of the sun
that the unknown birdcall of all of matter will reveal itself
& she will evolve to swallow the world of secret things

Acknowledgments

Thank you to the following publications in which versions of these poems were first published:

The Normal School: "walt whitman would be ashamed of you"
Organs of Vision and Speech: "poem for thomas jefferson"
Otis Nebula: "poem in belfast"

Note

"an assemblage of treasures in the treehouse" is after the New York Times article "Junkyard Poet of Whirligigs and Windmills" by Scott Shane (April 5, 2010).

Love & Gratitude to the following people for the careful eyes & minds, wise council & friendship you contributed to the writing of this book:

Nick Baranowski
Mary Brancaccio
Roberto Carlos Garcia
Brett Haymaker
Darla Himeles
Lynne McEniry
Yesenia Montilla
Sean Morrissey

…and to the following professors & mentors for their guidance early on:

Adrian Blevins
Ross Gay
Aracelis Girmay
Joan Larkin
Ira Sadoff
Judith Vollmer

…and to my family for their love & support